THE LIGHT OF CHRISTMAS

Reflections on the Season
of Advent and Christmas

Other books by Sheri A. Sutton

Memorable Moments
Sheri A. Sutton, 2016

In Remembrance of Me
Sheri A. Sutton, 2015

And So It Is
Westbow Press, 2013

THE LIGHT OF CHRISTMAS

Reflections on the Season
of Advent and Christmas

SHERI A. SUTTON

THE LIGHT OF CHRISTMAS

Reflections on the Season of Advent and Christmas

© 2014, 2016 Sheri A. Sutton

Second Edition

ISBN: 978-0-9984548-0-1

First Edition: Lighthouse Christian Publishing, 2014

Published by
Sheri A. Sutton
P.O. Box 22
Wichita Falls, Texas 76307
United States of America

www.sheriasutton.com

A SPECIAL THANK YOU...

to my daughter, Julie Yandell, for her insight and assistance.

TABLE OF CONTENTS

INTRODUCTION

Observed in many Christian churches, the Advent season signals our expectation and preparation for the birth of the Christ-child. The term advent is a version of the Latin word *adventus*, meaning "coming." It is this time period in the Christian religion that offers us the opportunity to share in the ancient longing for the coming of the Messiah and to anticipate his second coming as well.

Advent begins on the fourth Sunday before Christmas, which is the Sunday between November 27 and December 3, and ends on December 24. The reflections in this book assume the earliest beginning date of the season which gives us   twenty-eight Advent reflections followed by reflections for the Twelve Days of Christmas and Epiphany.

The Light of Christmas focuses on several themes dominant during the Advent season—hope, preparation, joy, and love. We *hope* for the fullness of God in our lives by our own intimate relationship with Jesus Christ. God is born within us through the birth of the Christ-child, and we *prepare* our minds and hearts for this experience just as God prepared the way to Bethlehem. When we experience the incredible gift of Christmas, we are filled with a deep, profound *joy* because we know with certainty that God's unconditional *love* is for each of us.

Although the Advent and Christmas season comes to an end, the presence of God still resides within us. As we recognize Christ within us, we can more readily recognize Christ in others. This *light* of Christmas is a flame that burns continuously. It is the flame that lights our path and empowers us to be the people that God created us to be. Most importantly, it reminds us that God is ever present in this moment and forevermore.

HOPE...

to expect with confidence

Psalm 33:22

May your unfailing love be with us, LORD, even as we put our hope in you.

We all hope for something—something expected to happen, or something longed for to happen, or something surprising to happen. During this time of Advent, we *expect* the birth of the Christ-child because we know that he holds for us the hope of salvation. We all need deliverance from the temptations and difficulties of life, and we hope for the fullness of that salvation through our faith and belief in Jesus Christ, the Son of the living God.

We also *long* for the coming of the Christ-child. There is something deep within each of us that calls out for the newness of life when everything is fresh and unspoiled. When you hold a baby, there is life pulsing in your arms with no expectations or pre-conceived ideas. In that moment, there is hope that a better world exists—a world full of light, peace, and love.

We hope for the *surprise* of Christmas in an unexpected gift, a gesture of friendship, or a word of love. Perhaps, however, the biggest surprise is discovering the baby Jesus within—God's gift of grace freely given to each of us, not when we are perfect, but when we are in need.

We wait in hope for the LORD; he is our help and our shield (v. 20).

Psalm 130:5
I wait for the LORD, my whole being waits, and in his word I put my hope.

Hope seems elusive especially in the middle of life's struggles. More often than not, we expect to solve all of our problems with limited thinking and inadequate resources. Scripture tells us that God is our hope, and sometimes we must wait for his guidance.

God is the creator of all things and the unlimited source for all questions. His understanding of any situation or circumstance is far beyond our understanding. When we make a decision or choice, it is based on our limited knowledge. However, God sees the whole picture, all parties involved, and all outcomes. If we are willing, he moves us forward with better results for our lives—all in his time.

The process is not always easy. We may question and not receive immediate answers, become afraid and take control, or give up five minutes before the miracle. Regardless of what we do, God remains faithful and is always engaged in offering hope to the hopeless, help to the helpless, and encouragement to the discouraged. Blessed are those whose hope, however small, is found in the Lord our God.

...put your hope in the LORD... (v. 7).

TUESDAY OF FIRST WEEK

Isaiah 7:14

Therefore the Lord himself will give you a sign: The virgin will conceive and give birth to a son, and will call him Immanuel.

From the beginning of time, God has wanted a relationship with his creation. And from the beginning of time, we have rebelled. The world is a deceitful place. It will tell us that God does not care and that he has abandoned us. But we have proof over and over again in Scripture that God exists and cares about his creation.

Immanuel in Hebrew means "God is with us." Even in the midst of our ordinary lives, God moves in us, around us, and through us. He shines his light in the dark corners of our lives, illuminates our path to keep us from stumbling, and ignites our spirits with the fire of his Spirit.

Every Christmas we celebrate the birth of Christ. God is born to us, dwells in us, and gives us life. Immanuel—*God is with us* wherever we are, even in a stable.

The people walking in darkness have seen a great light... (Isa. 9:2).

Isaiah 9:6

For to us a child is born, to us a son is given, and the government will be on his shoulders. And he will be called Wonderful Counselor, Mighty God, Everlasting Father, Prince of Peace.

Advent is the season of expectant waiting for the birth of the Christ-child. This time of the year offers us the opportunity to share in the ancient longing for the coming of the Messiah and to anticipate his return as well.

Deeply embedded in the Old Testament are many images of the promised Messiah. Various prophets spoke of a coming Savior, an expected ruler, and a new covenant. These prophets and others waited with expectancy—the state of hoping that something new and wonderful would happen. And something did.

On a star-filled night in Bethlehem, God in the flesh was revealed. It was an ordinary night that hosted the coming of the remarkable. In one amazing moment, God became man—the Messiah born for all humanity. In all of history, no other solitary life has affected the world as much as Jesus Christ. Today, more than two thousand years later, we still celebrate his birth. During this Advent season, we too eagerly anticipate the coming of the Christ-child.

Of the greatness of his government and peace there will be no end (v. 7).

Thursday of First Week

Malachi 3:1
"I will send my messenger, who will prepare the way before me.
Then suddenly the Lord you are seeking will come to his temple;
the messenger of the covenant, whom you desire, will come," says
the LORD Almighty.

We all receive messages in our daily lives from voice mails, texts, emails, and sometimes even snail mail. These messages may represent a note from a loved one, a reminder of an appointment, an invitation to a celebration, or a letter of thank you. Of course, we may also receive troubling messages concerning the loss of a loved one, a diagnosed illness, or an overdue payment. Messages can encourage us, bring us happiness, or send us spiraling into despair.

More than two thousand years ago, a man preached in the Desert of Judea and baptized his followers with water as an act for repentance. John the Baptist knew that he was the forerunner for the one who would baptize with the Holy Spirit. He brought the message of hope to those who had long awaited the coming of the Messiah.

Today we know that Christ came for each of us and brought God's message of love, forgiveness, and hope to all those who could hear. He still brings that same message today. The wait is over. The light overcomes the darkness, and the one we desire is here.

"...Return to me, and I will return to you," says the LORD Almighty
(v. 7).

Luke 3:15

The people were waiting expectantly and were all wondering in their hearts if John might possibly be the Messiah.

Waiting is not a fun pastime but is necessary in various circumstances. For example, we wait for the big wedding day. We wait for the birth of a child or grandchild. We wait for the opportunity that will change a job into a career. We wait for our children to leave home, and we wait for retirement. Life is a series of various periods of waiting.

People had been waiting expectantly for the Messiah. Was this man preaching in the desert the one that they had been waiting for? John the Baptist was adamant, "But one who is more powerful than I will come, the straps of whose sandals I am not worthy to untie" (v. 16).

Scripture tells us time and time again to wait. Wait for God's direction. Wait for God's plan. Wait for the power of the Holy Spirit. Wait...wait...wait for God's purpose to be revealed, for lives to be transformed, and for circumstances to change. Wait with hopeful confidence. The Christ is coming!

Now Jesus himself was about thirty years old when he began his ministry (v. 23).

John 1:4

In him was life, and that life was the light of all mankind.

God is light, and God is life. In choosing to believe in a power greater than ourselves, the Creator of the universe and all therein, we allow ourselves to walk in the light of truth, knowledge, and wisdom. When problems appear, we can view them in God's light and make choices based on his truth. We are free to move forward and are no longer bound to the darkness of fear and uncertainty. When we let our lives reflect the Christ within us, we have the opportunity to live a truly abundant life full of light, peace, and love.

Each morning as the sun rises in the east, the darkness of the night disappears, and a new day begins filled with light and life. This God-given day is ours to live fully and to shine God's light on all around us.

The light shines in the darkness, and the darkness has not overcome it (v. 5).

PREPARATION...

to make ready for an expected event

SECOND SUNDAY OF ADVENT

Matthew 1:16
...and Jacob the father of Joseph, the husband of Mary, and Mary was the mother of Jesus who is called the Messiah.

Genealogy involves tracing the lineages of families. It is most often used to demonstrate kinship and pedigrees of its members. Look at your family tree and marvel at the number of people from all different backgrounds that came together so that you could be here today.

The genealogy of Jesus was important to prove to Jewish leaders and believers that he had a right to the messianic throne. In Matthew's gospel, the lineage appears in three groups of fourteen as stated in Matthew 1:17, "Thus there were fourteen generations in all from Abraham to David, fourteen from David to the exile to Babylon, and fourteen from the exile to the Messiah." In this lineage, Joseph is reported as *the husband of Mary* who is reported as *the mother of Jesus*. Jesus, the Son of God, inherits his legal right to Israel's throne through his foster father, Joseph.

Old Testament prophets foretold the coming of the Messiah, and Jewish believers waited expectantly. All the while, God was preparing the way. On a starlit night in Bethlehem, God became flesh, and the prophecies were fulfilled.

...she was found to be pregnant through the Holy Spirit (v. 18).

Matthew 2:6
"'But you, Bethlehem, in the land of Judah, are by no means least among the rulers of Judah; for out of you will come a ruler who will shepherd my people Israel.'"

Identified as the birth place of Jesus, Bethlehem in Hebrew means "house of bread." For most people, bread is a staple food. For many, it is a daily struggle to provide this basic need for their families. However, in a spiritual sense, bread means much more than food for the body. It means nourishment for the soul. When the Israelites grumbled their way across the wilderness because they questioned God's daily provision, Moses reminded them that man does not live by bread alone but on God's word.

God became flesh that night in Bethlehem. In that moment, the hunger deep within our souls was satisfied for all eternity—no more darkness and no more fear. Written in 1867 by Phillip Brooks, the popular Christmas carol, *O Little Town of Bethlehem*, states it so eloquently: "Yet in thy dark streets shineth the everlasting Light; The hopes and fears of all the years are met in thee tonight."

Then Jesus declared, "I am the bread of life" (Jn. 6:35).

TUESDAY OF SECOND WEEK

Luke 1:13
But the angel said to him: "Do not be afraid, Zechariah; your prayer has been heard. Your wife Elizabeth will bear you a son, and you are to call him John."

Zechariah and Elizabeth were both well along in years and had no children as Elizabeth was barren. So when the angel appeared to Zechariah, he was somewhat skeptical to hear that his wife would bear him a son. However, God had a plan.

It was critical to prepare the way for the long-awaited Messiah. John the Baptist was living in the desert when he was called to be God's messenger. He went into all the countryside along the Jordan River with a message that focused on repentance, the forgiveness of sin, and the need for a Savior. Excitement ran high. Soon all mankind would witness God's salvation.

As we prepare for this Advent season, we still anticipate the coming of the Christ. Even now, over two thousand years later, we acknowledge our need for a Savior. Through the resurrecting power of God, we can be lifted from the grips of our transgressions into the light of his everlasting love.

"...for you will go on before the Lord to prepare the way for him..."
(v. 76).

Luke 1:30–31

But the angel said to her, "Do not be afraid, Mary; you have found favor with God. You will conceive and give birth to a son, and you are to call him Jesus."

As the angel approached Mary, he said that she was to give birth to a baby called Jesus, the Son of God. Mary was a godly young woman and lived her life in obedience to God. What was going through her mind? Was she thinking of the impact on her life? She was merely a humble woman from a lowly family. How could she be the mother of the Son of God? Was she fearful? How would she tell Joseph about the angel's message? Maybe she was excited. After all, she had been chosen to be the mother of Jesus.

We don't know the answers, but we do know one thing— Mary accepted God's will in her life. She would bring into the world the long-awaited Messiah. God had asked, and Mary had answered. Soon God would be revealed to all of humanity.

"So the holy one to be born will be called the Son of God" (v. 35).

Luke 2:4
So Joseph also went up from the town of Nazareth in Galilee to Judea, to Bethlehem the town of David, because he belonged to the house and line of David.

We can only imagine the impact of the journey to Bethlehem for Joseph and Mary. It was approximately ninety miles south of Nazareth to Bethlehem. They would have probably traveled along the flatlands of the Jordan River, turned west over the hills surrounding Jerusalem, and then on into Bethlehem. Most likely, they went no more than ten miles a day due to Mary's condition. It would have been a grueling trip. Winter in the Judean desert was cold and rainy, treacherous trails and roads would have been hard to maneuver, and desert pirates or wild animals might have added extra danger. They possibly carried bread and water with them because food would have been scarce.

What did they talk about as they traveled? Did they have questions about the child Mary was carrying? Did they speculate how their lives would change? Were they fearful? We do not know the answers to these questions or many others that could be posed. But we do know one thing—Joseph and Mary were obedient. God called them to be a part of his eternal plan, and they accepted.

While they were there, the time came for the baby to be born...
(v. 6).

FRIDAY OF SECOND WEEK

John 1:23
John replied in the words of Isaiah the prophet, "I am the voice of one calling in the wilderness, 'Make straight the way for the Lord.'"

During the holidays, our lives are filled with preparations. We decorate, we plan, and we shop. We anticipate with excitement all the activities associated with the holidays and pray that we will not forget someone's gift or burn the turkey.

The first Christmas did not happen by accident. God was busy preparing the way. Zechariah and Elizabeth's prayer had been heard. Elizabeth would bear a son, and he would be called John. John the Baptist would bear witness for the coming Messiah.

All important events in our lives require preparation. Each year as we prepare ourselves for the holidays, we also ready ourselves to receive God's greatest gift—the Christ-child. The birth of Jesus is not just significant during the Christmas holidays. It is significant every day. Through our belief in Jesus Christ as the Son of the living God, we are given the power of life to be born each day in the spirit of a child—a child who came with no fanfare or Christmas turkey. Most importantly, we have the opportunity every day for God to resurrect us from the darkness of struggle and despair into the light of truth and love.

He did not fail to confess, but confessed freely, "I am not the Messiah" (v. 20).

SATURDAY OF SECOND WEEK

1 Corinthians 2:9
However, as it is written: "What no eye has seen, what no ear has heard, and what no human mind has conceived"—the things God has prepared for those who love him....

It's hard to imagine the depth of God's love for us. Even so, he does love us more than we can imagine even when we fall short of his glory. He loves us because he created us. He knows us because he has searched our hearts. He liberates us because he is our redeemer. God's love for us began at the beginning of time and will be with us throughout eternity. Moreover, his purpose spans the past, present, and future and will be fully revealed in his time.

On a cold night in Bethlehem over two thousand years ago, a child was born. God's people had long awaited the coming of the one who would change the world. Were they truly ready for the Messiah? Perhaps. One thing was for certain. God was ready to live among us, to experience our humanness, and to give his life for each of us.

During this Advent season, let us ready ourselves for the coming of the Messiah. Let us open our hearts for God's love to permeate our bodies, minds, and spirits so that we can truly experience what he has prepared for us.

"For I know the plans I have for you," declares the LORD... (Jer. 29:11).

21

JOY...

delight, happiness, or bliss

THIRD SUNDAY OF ADVENT

Psalm 95:1
Come, let us sing for joy to the Lord; let us shout aloud to the Rock of our salvation.

Joy is a feeling of great happiness or delight. How do we find joy in a world that is filled with the problems that we all face on a daily basis?

There is a profound joy deep within our spirits that is present in a strong relationship with God. When we have God as our stronghold—our rock and our foundation—we have nothing to fear. We are empowered through God's power to push beyond our difficulties to experience a life that is happy, joyous, and free.

There will always be days of despair and disappointment. No one is exempt. However, there will also be days full of joy and happiness—a child's laugh, a family celebration, or a declaration of love. Let us celebrate this Advent and Christmas season with joy in our hearts and a song on our lips. In this moment, God is revealed to each of us through the birth of the Christ-child. What can be more joyful than that?

Come, let us bow down in worship...(v. 6).

Luke 1:44

"As soon as the sound of your greeting reached my ears, the baby in my womb leaped for joy."

Elizabeth was in the presence of something sacred. She knew for certain that God had called Mary to do the extraordinary, and she was filled with joy. When was the last time you were filled with joy?

Joy is an emotion that goes beyond the normal feeling of happiness to something deeper in one's spirit. Joy lights our eyes, fills our feet with dancing, and engulfs our spirit. It is deep within and is something that words cannot adequately describe. For example, think about the birth of a child. Everyone present is brought to tears. It is unexplainable the joy that is felt in that moment when the baby takes its first breath. Joy—profound, deep, and overwhelming. Once you have felt it, you will never forget it.

During the season of Advent and Christmas, we are reminded again of the precious gift that God gave us. In one stunning moment, God became human. The Christ-child was born, and the world changed forever. The joy that filled the air that night can still be felt today. When we open our hearts and let God be born within us, we too can experience the incredible gift of joy.

"Blessed is she who has believed that the Lord would fulfill his promises to her" (v. 45)!

Luke 2:10

But the angel said to them, "Do not be afraid. I bring you good news that will cause great joy for all the people."

Turn on the television or radio and listen to the news of the day. Not much is considered "good news" and certainly not news of "great joy." For the shepherds that night the news was different—a Savior had been born, the long awaited Messiah, the Christ.

A great company of angels appeared before the shepherds praising God. Imagine what they experienced—fear, excitement, amazement, or joy. Touched by what they had seen and heard, they hurried to find the baby. In a lowly stable in the town of Bethlehem, they found him lying in a manger. They told others what they had seen and returned to their fields glorifying and praising God.

The good news heard that night so long ago is still the good news for us today. No, we may not hear it on the nightly news, but we can hear it every day in our hearts. From the still small voice within, "The Christ is born. Open your heart and let him live within you. Acknowledge his presence and accept his grace. Do not be afraid. He is the good news!"

"Glory to God in the highest..." (v.14).

John 3:29

"The bride belongs to the bridegroom. The friend who attends the bridegroom waits and listens for him, and is full of joy when he hears the bridegroom's voice. That joy is mine, and it is now complete."

It is a sacred privilege to attend or to participate in a wedding ceremony. In this extraordinarily intimate moment, two people come together to pledge their love and support for one another in front of family members and friends who gather to celebrate and bless the union of the happy couple. Weddings are joyful—full of laughter and full of tears.

Whether a close friend or a family member, the best man plays a specific role in the festivities of a wedding. His duty is to support and assist the groom, the most important male participant in the ceremony. The relationship of these two men is such that the best man is filled with joy and celebrates the new life that awaits the groom.

And so it was with John the Baptist. He came to publicly proclaim the coming of the Messiah. He came to prepare the way for a new way of life for all those who would believe. He came so that his joy, and our joy, would be complete.

"He must become greater; I must become less" (v. 30).

John 16:21

"A woman giving birth to a child has pain because her time has come; but when her baby is born she forgets the anguish because of her joy that a child is born into the world."

Mothers know the pain referenced in the above verse, and they also know that the memory of that pain slips away with time. What is left is the joy they felt when they first looked upon that angelic face.

In the verse above, Jesus explained to the disciples that they would feel extreme grief when he was no longer with them. He also said that their mourning would turn into a joy that no one could take away. In our relationship with God, there is an eternal joy that permeates our being and propels us forward even when we despair.

That joy began on a cold winter's night centuries ago when a baby was born for all mankind. The Christ-child brought to this world a joy that cannot be defined. As we develop our relationship with God through our belief in Jesus Christ, that joy grows immeasurably more than we can ever imagine—a joy deep within our hearts spurred by God's amazing love for each of us.

"Ask and you will receive, and your joy will be complete" (v. 24).

FRIDAY OF THIRD WEEK

Romans 15:12–13

And again, Isaiah says, "The Root of Jesse will spring up, one who will arise to rule over the nations; in him the Gentiles will hope." May the God of hope fill you with all joy and peace as you trust in him....

In 1734, Alexander Pope wrote in his *An Essay on Man*, "Hope springs eternal in the human breast." For all believers, hope is indeed what we hold dear in our hearts. Hope is that spark, that flicker of a flame, which shines deep within our spirits and fills us with intense joy and peace.

For centuries, people had anticipated with great expectation the coming of the Messiah. They had hoped for a better world and a better life. Most importantly, they had hoped that God would not forsake them. And God didn't.

During this season of Advent and Christmas, we are reminded once again of that night in Bethlehem when God's undying love for his creation became visible. Joy and peace filled the air and the hearts of mankind. In one remarkable moment, God looked upon the world through the eyes of a child, and the world changed forever.

...you removed my sackcloth and clothed me with joy... (Ps. 30:11).

Galatians 5:22–23
But the fruit of the Spirit is love, joy, peace, forbearance, kindness, goodness, faithfulness, gentleness and self-control. Against such things there is no law.

In Jesus' teachings to the disciples, he spoke about the fruit of the vine. If the branches (the followers) remained with the vine (Jesus), then the branches would bear much fruit. In the verse above, Paul lists joy as a fruit or outgrowth of our relationship with God through Jesus Christ.

Relationships offer us opportunities for great joy, but they also offer us opportunities for great pain. When we are in relationship with another, there is always the possibility that the person will say or do something that will be devastating to our spirits. Perhaps, an unkind word is spoken, a lie is told, or a promise is broken. Those acts can certainly take away our joy. However, in a relationship with God, his promises and truth are never compromised.

God was born into the world so that we might experience him as we had never experienced him before. He came as a light in the darkness to transform our lives with his mercy and grace. Moreover, he came so that we would know a joy found only in his never-ending faithfulness and everlasting love.

Since we live by the Spirit, let us keep in step with the Spirit (v. 25).

LOVE...

strong affection and devotion to another

FOURTH SUNDAY OF ADVENT

Psalm 63:3
Because your love is better than life, my lips will glorify you.

In Psalm 63, the psalmist confesses his longing for God's presence in his life. He knows that a close personal relationship with God will offer a joy not found anywhere else. Why? God is love. There is no other love greater than the love of God. He loves us unconditionally. He loves us not because of what we do but because of who we are—his creation. He loves us with abandon and freely offers us his gift of grace.

When God came into the world, he came to show his love for us so that we could offer that love to others. The love of God empowers the powerless, uplifts the downtrodden, and sustains the tired and weary. God's love offers hope—a belief that love conquers all fears, overcomes the impossible, and resurrects us from the darkness of unbelief.

During this last week of Advent, let us focus on God's love for each of us. Let us focus on the transforming power of that love and then offer it to those around us. Let us be the catalyst that brings the love of Christmas into the world.

I will praise you as long as I live, and in your name I will lift up my hands (v. 4).

MONDAY OF FOURTH WEEK

Psalm 100:5

For the Lord is good and his love endures forever; his faithfulness continues through all generations.

Forever is a hard concept to comprehend. In today's world where everything is instant, temporary, and disposable, the concept of forever seems somewhat obsolete. So how can we understand the meaning of forever?

Look up into the night sky. Gaze beyond every glittering star and imagine the depth of the universe, or look beyond the ocean shore and contemplate the deepness of the sea. Words cannot adequately describe it. Our minds cannot fully comprehend it. In the infinite vastness there is forever.

On a starry night in Bethlehem, God came into the world so that we might know his love—a love that spans the past, present, and future. God's love empowers us, sustains us, and protects us. It transforms our lives and brings healing to a broken world. God has promised us his love, and it is his commitment to us...forever.

...give thanks to him and praise his name (v. 4).

Matthew 3:17

And a voice from heaven said, "This is my Son, whom I love; with him I am well pleased."

Fathers and sons have an interesting dynamic. In many cases, sons emulate their fathers by developing the same habits, interests, and careers. Regardless of the situation, the underlying desire of the son is the love and respect of the father.

When we develop a relationship with God, we want to become like him. We want to follow his guidance, to acquire his character, and to love as he loves. God's love allows us to forgive, to conquer fear, and to live peacefully. It mends the brokenness of our lives and restores us to wholeness. It empowers us to move forward, to take risks, and to recreate our lives. Love is the best vehicle through which God is revealed.

When we extend our hand in love and fellowship, even to our enemies, we are extending God's hand. Perhaps in that moment we will hear God whisper, "This is my child whom I love and am well pleased."

"They knew with certainty that I came from you, and they believed that you sent me" (Jn. 17:8).

John 3:16
For God so loved the world that he gave his one and only Son, that whoever believes in him shall not perish but have eternal life.

When God created the world and all therein, he saw that it was good, and he was well pleased. However, as in all stories, the plot took a turn. Man rebelled. In Scripture, we read the accounts of man's struggle with his separation from God and subsequent dependence on God. It is as if man, left to his own devices, will always rebel until he is knocked to his knees in total surrender.

Since the beginning of time, God has wanted a relationship with his creation. Although we have denied him and rejected him time and time again, he still pursues us with a passion because he loves us. He loves us so much that he came to live among us.

Centuries ago, a child was born. He brought the world a love like no one had ever experienced. He brought us light to fill the darkness. He brought us peace to fill our spirits. He brought us the promise of everlasting life. God was in our midst, and the world would never be the same.

"Light has come into the world..." (v. 19).

THURSDAY OF FOURTH WEEK

John 15:9
"As the Father has loved me, so have I loved you. Now remain in my love."

Remain means to stay (do not leave) or linger (delay leaving). In the verse above, Jesus tells us to *stay* in his love. Why? When we remain in God's love, we find comfort, peace, and grace. Furthermore, because love is transforming, extraordinary things can happen.

Love can take us from the darkness of despair into the light of hope. It can change our attitudes and perceptions, restore relationships, rebuild families, heal the sick, and feed the hungry. Love is a power beyond all other powers. It is the power of God.

When we remain in God's love, we are empowered to change the world. We are strengthened to complete God's call on our lives. Moreover, we are elevated to forgive those who have hurt us. God came to give us life—a life full of his everlasting love.

"...apart from me you can do nothing" (v. 5).

FRIDAY OF FOURTH WEEK

Romans 8:38–39

For I am convinced that neither death nor life, neither angels nor demons, neither the present nor the future, nor any powers, neither height nor depth, nor anything else in all creation, will be able to separate us from the love of God that is in Christ Jesus our Lord.

Life separates us in many ways. An illness, divorce, or death can take away family and friends with no notice or warning. Many times we are left to grieve and mourn alone.

The above verse tells us that we are never separated from the love of God. There is not anything, not even death, which disconnects us from our Creator. Imagine it. No separation, no isolation, and no condemnation. God is available at any time of the day. He gives us comfort when we grieve. He gives us strength when we struggle. He gives us power when we are powerless. Most importantly, he gives us love.

In the birth of the Christ-child, God's love was presented as never before. The baby offered a new beginning and a new way of life. The long awaited Messiah had made his appearance. He came to live among us, to be in relationship with us, and to give us eternal and everlasting love.

No, in all these things we are more than conquerors through him who loved us (v. 37).

Ephesians 3:17–19

And I pray that you, being rooted and established in love, may have power, together with all the Lord's holy people, to grasp how wide and long and high and deep is the love of Christ, and to know this love that surpasses knowledge—that you may be filled to the measure of all the fullness of God.

In plants, the root system usually lies below the surface of the ground and, although not seen, is extremely important to the growth of the plant. The four basic functions of a root system are absorption of water and nutrients, storage of nutrients, the anchoring and support of the plant, and vegetative reproduction. For a plant to be healthy and productive there must be a strong and vigorous root system. It is the same in our relationship with God.

There are no words that adequately describe the depth of God's love for each of us. It is beyond our comprehension and our scope of reference. For our lives to be productive and healthy, we must be strongly rooted in this love. Only then can we open our hearts and minds to his principles and teachings, store his promises in our hearts, overcome the storms of life, and produce the fruits of the Spirit.

When God came into the world on that night so long ago, he came to give us hope. He came to give us purpose. Most importantly, he came to give us his light, peace, and love so that we might *be filled to the measure of all the fullness of God.*

...according to his power that is at work within us... (v. 20).

THE TWELVE DAYS OF CHRISTMAS

Christ—God incarnate, the Messiah

44

Luke 2:6–7
While they were there, the time came for the baby to be born, and she gave birth to her firstborn, a son. She wrapped him in cloths and placed him in a manger, because there was no guest room available for them.

Stables, buildings used for the shelter and feeding of animals such as horses and cattle, are not the cleanest places and have a distinct odor that is overwhelming at times. Nevertheless, that is where Jesus made his entrance into this world.

In the midst of dirty conditions, God was revealed in the birth of a baby—a sign of life and pure love. On that star-filled night over two thousand years ago, those present experienced a miracle. In a stable amid the hay, the animals, and the stench, the heavens proclaimed God's gift to the world.

As we once again celebrate the birth of the Christ-child, we have the opportunity to ground ourselves in the power of the living God. God came into the world for each of us. He came to bring us life when we are dead in spirit, hope when we are in despair, light when we are in darkness, love when we are unlovable, peace when we are in conflict, and forgiveness when we fall short. These gifts are given to each of us through God's grace. May this Christmas day open our eyes to God's power and presence, and may we see the miracle of the Christ-child in the most unexpected places.

Today in the town of David a Savior has been born to you; he is the Messiah, the Lord (v. 11).

SECOND DAY OF CHRISTMAS

Isaiah 60:1
"Arise, shine, for your light has come, and the glory of the Lord rises upon you."

The morning sunrise is breathtaking. Slowly, the sun rises over the horizon, and the darkness of the night begins to retreat. Gradually, the sunlight becomes brighter and awakens the new day. Dew sparkles as sunbeams jump across blades of grass, flowers lift their heads to bask in the warmth of the sun, and wildlife venture out to find their first meal of the day. All of creation is awakened to the possibilities of a new beginning.

God does that for us. He brings us out of the darkness and into the light where we can see infinite possibilities. Our struggles always seem more urgent and foreboding in the dark. When we ask God to be a part of our lives, he dispels the darkness and awakens us with his light, peace, and love.

For more than two thousand years, people have believed that Christ is the light of the world. God incarnate, born for humanity's salvation, came to give us light—the light that overcomes all darkness, that offers hope, and that illuminates our path. The Bethlehem star that shone so brightly on that night long ago still shines just as vibrantly on us today. Awake and see the light!

...but the LORD rises upon you and his glory appears over you (v. 2).

46

Ecclesiastes 3:10–11

I have seen the burden God has laid on the human race. He has made everything beautiful in its time. He has also set eternity in the human heart; yet no one can fathom what God has done from beginning to end.

God makes everything beautiful in its time. As humans, it is difficult to wait for God's purpose to be revealed. We want to know the outcome today—not tomorrow, or next week, or next year. We yearn to know, and we worry that our lives won't turn out the way we imagine.

Look at a rose bush. It is planted, watered, and given needed nutrients. Slowly, rose buds begin to appear covered tightly with green leaf-like structures that protect the developing buds. Over time, the buds begin to open, and eventually full roses are revealed. Beautiful roses do not develop overnight, and neither do our lives.

God's plan for humanity began before the creation of the world. Part of that plan was revealed on a starry night long ago. The Christ-child, God incarnate, came into the world. He came to live among us, to show us his love, and to give us salvation. God's plan is not finished. He has a purpose for each of us, and that purpose will be revealed in his time.

There is a time for everything... (v. 1).

Fourth Day of Christmas

John 1:18

No one has ever seen God, but the one and only Son, who is himself God and is in closest relationship with the Father, has made him known.

Many situations show us the existence of God—a newborn baby, the beauty of nature, the vastness of the universe, the wide open plains, or the deepness of the oceans. However, to *see* God, we must first see Jesus.

After hundreds of years of trying to be in relationship with man, God came to earth as Jesus, the Son of God and the Son of Man. He came to bring the light of truth and the promise of life. Moreover, he came to bear witness to God's amazing love and grace.

Look at Jesus, and you will see the Father—loving, compassionate, and full of grace. Study the life of Jesus, and you will see complete obedience to God's will, even when it led to the cross. Listen closely to the teacher, and you will hear the Father's words of truth and power. Watch the healer, and you will see God transforming the body, mind, and spirit. Look closely at Jesus, and you will *see* God.

For the Father loves the Son and shows him all he does (Jn. 5:20).

FIFTH DAY OF CHRISTMAS

John 8:12

When Jesus spoke again to the people, he said, "I am the light of the world. Whoever follows me will never walk in darkness, but will have the light of life."

On the first day of creation, God said, "Let there be light" (Gen. 1:3). Light is magical. It makes darkness disappear and is essential for growth. Sunlight brings warmth on cold wintry days and boosts our spirits. Light enhances our lives.

God came into the world to bring light to those in darkness, hope to those in despair, and life to those dead in spirit. His light illuminates our path, brightens our day, and gives us peace. It is essential for our growth, and it is transforming.

The star of Bethlehem shined brightly those many years ago and welcomed into the world the Son of God. That light, the light of Christ, still shines ever so brightly today. It is our beacon when we are lost. It is our strength when we are weak. Moreover, it is our salvation when we are in need.

God saw that the light was good, and he separated the light from the darkness (Gen. 1:4).

SIXTH DAY OF CHRISTMAS

John 12:44

Then Jesus cried out, "Whoever believes in me does not believe in me only, but in the one who sent me."

What is belief? By definition, belief is a conviction of the truth or the reality of something. Beliefs are established during our lifetime and are usually based on our experience and upbringing. Many beliefs are subject to change, but our core beliefs set the foundation for our lives.

For believers everywhere, Jesus is the Son of God. If that is indeed our foundational belief, then it follows that we can also believe in the one who sent Jesus. What does that belief offer us? God empowers us. He resurrects us from the abyss of despair. He heals our brokenness. He renews our spirits and changes our hearts. God moves in us, around us, and through us and transforms our lives.

As we celebrate the Christmas season, we celebrate not only the birth of Christ but also God's presence in our lives. We celebrate his joy, light, and peace. God, who created the universe and breathed life into man, reminds us through the Christ-child that he is real, alive, and active in our lives today.

"The one who looks at me is seeing the one who sent me" (v. 45).

SEVENTH DAY OF CHRISTMAS

DECEMBER 31

John 17:3
Now this is eternal life: that they know you, the only true God, and Jesus Christ, whom you have sent.

Eternal means without end, forever, and existing at all times. Eternal life is never-ending life. According to the verse above, we receive eternal life through knowing God; and we come to know God through Jesus Christ.

God creates life. He sustains life, and he transforms life. God is life, and he pulses through our veins every moment. In sharing life with God, we overcome the power of death and are freed from the shackles of this world. We are liberated to live happy, joyous, and free.

As we contemplate the meaning of Christmas, let us concentrate on life. God came into the world as new life, without fanfare or parades. He came to know us so that we could know him. He came to love us so that we could love him. He came to resurrect our spirits and transform our lives. Most importantly, he came to give us eternal, never-ending life.

They knew with certainty that I came from you, and they believed that you sent me (v. 8).

EIGHTH DAY OF CHRISTMAS

JANUARY 1

2 Corinthians 4:6
For God, who said, "Let light shine out of darkness," made his light shine in our hearts to give us the light of the knowledge of God's glory displayed in the face of Christ.

During creation as explained in the first chapter of Genesis, we know that God called forth light and separated it from darkness. We also know God saw that everything was good. In the Gospel of John, we learn that the Word (Jesus) was with God in the beginning and through him everything was formed. We can determine, therefore, that the Word is the very essence of light, goodness, and beauty.

When Jesus was born into the world, it was a message to all mankind of God's love for his creation. God loved us enough to come to us in the flesh, to walk with us through life's difficulties, to lift us up when we are downtrodden, and to create within us a desire for change.

Thousands of years have passed since the creation of the universe, but the light that God created in the beginning is still vibrant today. More than two thousand years ago, God in the flesh was born. He came to shine his eternal light for all mankind. He came to teach us the truth. He came to show us his love in the midst of life's messiness and chaos. Most of all, he came to release our spirits so that we can live fully and unafraid.

The Son is the radiance of God's glory... (Heb. 1:3).

52

Galatians 4:4–5
But when the set time had fully come, God sent his Son, born of a woman, born under the law, to redeem those under the law, that we might receive adoption to sonship.

"Sonship" in the days of Paul was a socially significant term. In those days, a young child of a wealthy family was placed in the care of a slave. This family slave was responsible for the child's care and discipline. In due time, the child was legally recognized as a "son" and was freed from the control of the family slave.

God had a plan on that night so long ago. A baby was born, but he was no ordinary baby. He was the Son of God. He came to redeem us and to liberate us. He came so that we might know our Father up close and personal.

Through our belief in Jesus Christ, God receives us into his family and fully recognizes us as his sons and daughters. In doing so, we are heirs to the resurrecting power of God that transforms and empowers our lives.

So you are no longer a slave, but God's child... (v. 7).

Philippians 2:9–10

Therefore God exalted him to the highest place and gave him the name that is above every name, that at the name of Jesus every knee should bow, in heaven and on earth and under the earth....

If you want to get someone's attention, speak his or her name. Calling someone by name is an effective tool in communication. Why does a name hold such power? A name identifies a thing or person and gives it recognition and authority. A personal name distinguishes individuals from one another, whereas a specific product name identifies a particular marketable item. Every created thing on earth is differentiated by its own unique name giving it identification and authenticity.

Scripture tells us of one name above all other names that is filled with God's resurrecting power—Jesus. It can deliver us from unhealthy lifestyles, the darkness of grief, the despair of loneliness, and the trap of anger and resentment. It can heal our bodies, minds, and spirits. By repeating it often, it will comfort us, bring us peace, and offer us hope. If we let it permeate our hearts and occupy our minds, we will know its power—Jesus, the name above all others.

...and every tongue acknowledge that Jesus Christ is Lord, to the glory of God the Father (v. 11).

ELEVENTH DAY OF CHRISTMAS

Revelation 3:20
Here I am! I stand at the door and knock. If anyone hears my voice and opens the door, I will come in and eat with that person, and they with me.

Have you ever ignored someone knocking at your door? Perhaps you have slept late, or you are in the middle of a project, or you just do not want to be disturbed. Most likely, we all do it sometimes. Ignore it, and it will go away.

God knocks on the door to our hearts. He waits patiently for us to answer. Do we keep working? Do we ignore that someone is there? Do we ever open the door? Perhaps we are anxious. We may believe that God will ask us to do something we do not want to do, or that he will want to stay longer than we have time, or that he will ask us to give up something we hold dear. It is the human dilemma—fear of the unknown.

On that first Christmas night, God knocked on the hearts of all mankind. In that moment, he offered us life with meaning and direction. He offered us love for all eternity, and he offered us hope to overcome fear. All we need to do is open the door.

...so that when he comes and knocks they can immediately open the door for him (Lk. 12:36).

55

TWELFTH DAY OF CHRISTMAS

Revelation 21:3
"God's dwelling place is now among the people, and he will dwell with them. They will be his people, and God himself will be with them and be their God."

The Christmas season has come and gone. Out of town guests have traveled back to their homes, Christmas decorations have been put away, and the home has been returned to its normal state. All signs of Christmas have disappeared. Well...maybe not all signs.

When God came to humanity as Jesus, he came to live with us and to commune with us. He came to shine his light in the dark corners of our lives. He came to love us when no one else cares. He came to grant us mercy and forgiveness when we fall short and to liberate us from the yoke of fear.

When Christmas is over, God does not leave us. He is with us as we live our daily lives. He celebrates with us, cries with us, encourages us, and comforts us. He is with us when we question and when we doubt. He loves us with abandon and seeks to bring us home when we stray. God dwells among us and is with us always. We are his people, and he is our God.

He said to me: "It is done. I am the Alpha and the Omega, the Beginning and the End" (v. 6).

EPIPHANY...

a sudden and striking realization

EPIPHANY

Matthew 2:11

On coming to the house, they saw the child with his mother Mary, and they bowed down and worshiped him. Then they opened their treasures and presented him with gifts of gold, frankincense and myrrh.

There are numerous events and special days which happen during one's lifetime that we celebrate with gifts. These presents usually have a meaning or significance depending on the giver, the recipient, or the event being celebrated. However, the best present is always the unexpected.

The Magi, a class of wise men, came from the East to Jerusalem several months after Jesus' birth. The journey was long, but they believed God's promises and went in search of the newborn king of the Jews. These men of faith came with no hidden agenda, only overwhelming joy. Upon finding the baby, they bowed in worship and offered gifts fitting a king.

Mary and Joseph didn't expect gifts when Jesus was born. They were probably still in awe of the shepherds' visit. So when the Magi came bearing the type of gifts given to royalty, Mary and Joseph were probably speechless. However, the most wondrous gift that special day was not the gifts *from* the Magi but the gift *to* the Magi—bowing in worship before the long-awaited Messiah. They had witnessed the Christ-child, the Son of God.

When they saw the star, they were overjoyed (v. 10).

JOHN 12:46

I have come into the world as a light, so that no one who believes in me should stay in darkness.

BLESSING

If you are reading this page, then it probably means that you made it through this book. Hopefully, it has touched your heart and helped you to see this holiday season in a new *light*. It also means that the festivities are behind you. Your family has gathered for their traditional celebration, packages have been opened, gifts have been exchanged, and the leftover turkey has made its last showing on the dinner table.

Perhaps, amid all the hustle and bustle of this Advent and Christmas season, you have experienced the presence of the Christ-child in the eyes of your child or grandchild, or in the embrace of a family member or friend, or even in the casual meeting of a stranger. Maybe in the stillness of the early morning amid meditation and prayer, you have encountered the Son of God like never before and felt his power in the deepest part of your spirit. Although the holidays are behind us and we return to the ordinary activities of living, the Christ-child still dwells with us every day.

Over two thousand years ago, a brilliant star shone over a stable in Bethlehem. That star was a sign to all who saw it that the Christ-child—the Messiah—had indeed come into the world. He came to give us life and hope. He came to give us love and peace. He came to give us forgiveness and grace. May the *light* of that star shine for you throughout this coming year, and may *"the Lord bless you and keep you; the Lord make his face shine on you and be gracious to you; the Lord turn his face toward you and give you peace"* (Num. 6:24-26).

ABOUT THE AUTHOR

Sheri A. Sutton is an author, devotional writer, and poet. *The Light of Christmas* is the second of three devotional books and is a collection of meditations for the season of Advent and Christmas. In addition, her devotional writing has been published in the *Secret Place* devotional magazine and the *Lenten Devotions on the Lord's Prayer.*

As a member of the Wichita Falls Poetry Society and the Poetry Society of Texas, Sutton has been recognized in various contests. Her poetry has been published in the *Wichita Falls Literature and Art Review* magazine, The Poetry Society of Texas' *A Book of the Year, Lifting the Sky,* and her latest work, *Memorable Moments.*

For a limited time, she wrote a monthly newspaper column while serving on the Community Editorial Board of the Times Record News.

Sutton also offers professional services that include writing and editing for books, newsletters, and other materials for individuals, companies, or organizations. Visit her website, www.sheriasutton.com, for more information.

Sutton and her husband, Lloyd Mark Sutton, live in Wichita Falls, Texas.

Made in the USA
Columbia, SC
08 December 2023